Ferdinand Küchler (1867 – 1937)
Concertino

in the style of | im Stil von | dans le style d'
Antonio Vivaldi

for Violin and Piano
für Violine und Klavier
pour violon et piano

D major | D-Dur | Ré majeur

opus 15

Edited by | Herausgegeben von | Edité par
Wolfgang Birtel

Edited, with Preface and Teaching Notes by
Herausgegeben mit einem Vorwort und Hinweisen für den Unterricht von
Edité, avec préface et indications pour l'apprentissage par
Peter Mohrs

Level | Schwierigkeitsgrad D/USA: 2 UK/AUS: 4

SE 1042
ISMN 979-0-001-16728-4

▶ **MP3 play-along separately available:**
www.schott-student-edition.com

Mainz · London · Berlin · Madrid · New York · Paris · Prague · Tokyo · Toronto
© 2019 SCHOTT MUSIC GmbH & Co. KG, Mainz · Printed in Germany

Preface

There are pieces that have figured in the standard violin teaching repertoire for decades: enjoyable for students to play as fundamental technical and musical challenges are introduced, these pieces rank as essential tuition material. One such piece is this Concertino in D major op. 15 by Küchler, which – along with Küchler's Concertino op. 11 in G major (Schott SE 1001) and Oskar Rieding's Concertino op. 35 in B minor (Schott SE 1027) – is one of the most popular and most often played concertos ever written for students.

Ferdinand Küchler was hugely influential as a violin teacher and composer of tuition repertoire; born in Giessen on 14.7.1867, he died in Leipzig on 24.10.1937.
Küchler studied violin at the Hoch Conservatoire in Frankfurt from 1883–1888. From 1889 he played viola in an orchestra and a string quartet in Basle, where he was also director of his own music school from 1911. He then taught at the Leipzig Conservatoire from 1927–1937. Küchler's violin tutorial books and his dedication to training string players had a significant influence on violin teaching methods.

The Concertino op. 15 'in the style of Antonio Vivaldi' quickly captivates the hearts and fingers of young violinists with the lively impetus of its outer movements and expressive melodies in the slow middle movement. Like all Küchler's compositions, it nevertheless bears the hallmark of the experienced string player: every note is written for the instrument, lying well under the fingers with music that is simply fun to play.

In comparison with the original edition of 1937, the score has been pared down with regard to articulation and adapted to match the modern approach to Baroque pieces. This allows each player to work out their own individual interpretation: further details will be found in the *Teaching Notes*.

Have fun learning to play this lovely concerto!

Peter Mohrs
Translation Julia Rushworth

Vorwort

Es gibt Stücke, die gehören seit Jahrzehnten zum Standardrepertoire der Violinpädagogik und sind aus dem Unterricht nicht mehr wegzudenken, weil sie den Schülern Spaß machen und daran grundlegende technische und musikalische Aufgabenstellungen erlernt werden können. Dies gilt auch für das vorliegende Concertino in D-Dur op. 15 von Küchler. Das Werk zählt – neben Küchlers Concertino op. 11 in G-Dur (Schott SE 1001) und Oskar Riedings Concertino op. 35 in h-Moll (Schott SE 1027) – zu den beliebtesten und meistgespielten Schülerkonzerten überhaupt.

Ferdinand Küchler, geb. am 14.7.1867 in Gießen, gest. am 24.10.1937 in Leipzig, gehört zu den bedeutendsten Violinpädagogen und Komponisten von Unterrichtsliteratur. Er studierte von 1883–1888 Violine am Hoch'schen Konservatorium in Frankfurt, wirkte ab 1889 in Basel als Bratscher im Orchester und in einem Streichquartett, ab 1911 auch als Leiter einer eigenen Musikschule. Von 1927–1937 unterrichtete er am Leipziger Konservatorium. Mit seiner Violinschule und durch seine Arbeit in der Streicherausbildung hat Küchler die Violinpädagogik maßgeblich geprägt.

Das Concertino op. 15 „im Stil von Antonio Vivaldi" überzeugt durch seine motorischen, spritzigen Ecksätze sowie durch die ausdrucksvolle Melodik des langsamen Mittelsatzes und erobert sehr rasch Finger und Herzen der jungen Geigerinnen und Geiger. Dabei lässt es, wie alle Kompositionen Küchlers, die Handschrift des erfahrenen Streichers erkennen. Alles ist für das Instrument geschrieben, liegt gut in der Hand und es macht einfach Freude, diese Musik zu spielen.

Gegenüber der originalen Ausgabe von 1937 wurde der Notentext hinsichtlich der Artikulation „verschlankt" und dem heutigen Standard für barocke Werke angepasst. Es erleichtert dem Spieler seine eigene Interpretation zu finden. Mehr dazu in den *Hinweisen für den Unterricht*.

Viel Freude beim Einstudieren dieses schönen Konzerts!

Peter Mohrs

Préface

Certains morceaux font partie du répertoire pédagogique standard du violon depuis des décennies et il est inimaginable qu'ils en disparaissent. En effet, les élèves les jouent avec plaisir et ont par la même occasion la possibilité de s'approprier des fondamentaux techniques et musicaux. Il en va ainsi du concertino en ré majeur op. 15 de Küchler. Au côté du concertino op. 11 en sol majeur de Küchler (Schott SE 1001) et du concertino op. 35 en si mineur d'Oskar Rieding (Schott SE 1027), cette œuvre compte parmi les concertos à vocation pédagogique les plus appréciés et les plus souvent joués.

Né le 14.7.1867 à Giessen et mort le 24.10.1937 à Leipzig, Ferdinand Küchler est l'un des pédagogues du violon et des compositeurs de répertoire pédagogique pour cet instrument les plus significatifs. Après avoir étudié le violon au conservatoire Hoch à Francfort entre 1883 et 1888, il exerça à Bâle dès 1889 en tant qu'altiste au sein de l'orchestre et dans un quatuor, tout en dirigeant sa propre école de musique à partir de 1911. Entre 1927 et 1937, il enseigna au conservatoire de Leipzig. Par sa méthode de violon et son travail en faveur de la formation des instrumentistes à cordes, Küchler a marqué profondément la pédagogie du violon.

Le concertino op. 15 « dans le style d'Antonio Vivaldi » convainc autant par le caractère vif et animé de ses mouvements extrêmes que par la mélodie expressive du mouvement lent central et conquiert très vite les doigts et les cœurs des jeunes violonistes. Comme dans toutes les compositions de Küchler, la patte d'un instrumentiste à cordes expérimenté y est perceptible. Tout est écrit pour l'instrument et vient bien sous les doigts. Jouer cette musique est tout simplement un plaisir.

Par rapport à l'édition originale de 1937, la partition a été « débroussaillée » ici du point de vue de l'articulation et ajustée aux normes utilisées actuellement pour les œuvres baroques afin de permettre à l'instrumentiste de trouver plus facilement sa propre interprétation. Pour davantage de détails à ce propos, se reporter aux *Indications pour l'apprentissage*.

Régalez-vous avec ce beau concerto !

Peter Mohrs
Traduction Michaëla Rubi

Concertino
in the style of / im Stil von / dans le style d'
Antonio Vivaldi
opus 15

Ferdinand Küchler
1867–1937

I

© 2019 Schott Music GmbH & Co. KG, Mainz

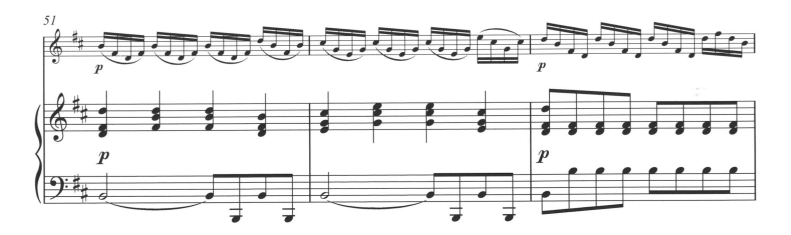

58

62

allargando

allargando

II Siciliano

Larghetto (♪ ca. 82)

p ma espressivo

p

5

mf

mf

p *f*

p *f*

31

34

38

42

46

49

51

53

55

58

62

II Siciliano

III Allegro assai

senza allargando

Schott Music, Mainz 59 142

Concertino
in the style of / im Stil von / dans le style d'
Antonio Vivaldi
opus 15

Ferdinand Küchler
1867–1937

I

SE 1042

Adagio

attacca subito

III Allegro assai

Allegro assai (♩. ca. 64)

69

77

85

93
senza allargando

senza allargando

Schott Music, Mainz 59 142

Teaching Notes

Among the four Concertinos by Küchler, this Concertino op. 15 'in the style of Antonio Vivaldi' stands out immediately for its style of composition: where Küchler used a Classical-Romantic musical language in his other little concertos for students, here he writes a work in Baroque style that, to a wide extent, suggests a composition by Vivaldi.

The theme in the first movement (*Allegro moderato*) immediately presents echoes of the famous Concerto in A minor op. 3/6 by the Italian composer and violin teacher, as repeated notes characterise the theme in both violin concertos. There are also parallels with regard to form, using the alternation of a recurring *ritornello* section with solo sections typical of Vivaldi. Several exuberant sixteenth note (semiquaver) runs also exude the spirit of Vivaldi. Besides 1st position, these runs require 3rd position in a few places. While the title page of the first edition specifies '1st and 3rd position', it may make sense to use 2nd position occasionally, for instance in bar 29 of the first movement, and in some places in the slow movement, too. Mastery of the first three fingering patterns is required, with nimble fingers and confident bowing.

The slow second movement (*Larghetto*) with the lilting 6/8 time of a *Siciliano* provides a wonderful contrast. It also has a few passages using 3rd position and with many gentle slurs calling for lyrical playing, the focus shifts more to the bowing arm and musical phrasing.

The third movement (*Allegro assai*) is a merrily effervescent Rondo in 3/8 time, calling for clear emphasis on the first two beats in the bar. Here, too, several passages in 3rd position will require special attention. This Rondo calls for fluent playing at speed and a flexible right wrist.

Ferdinand Küchler marked the violin part for his Concertino 'in the style of Antonio Vivaldi' with very precise articulation, with notable use of *portato* and *staccato* marking. This reflects the style fashionable at the end of the 19th Century and beginning of the 20th Century. Questions as to how music of the Baroque age should be interpreted and performed have been answered in various ways over the course of time, reflecting changing fashions for interpretation in the spirit of each era. Many things will be played differently now than in Küchler's time, drawing on modern insights into historical performance practice. It has therefore been decided with this new edition not to reproduce Küchler's articulation markings, but to use the sparser notation that was customary in the Baroque era, giving violinists access to a clearer picture of the music, while some bowings and fingerings have been added.

Of course we must bear in mind the fact that Küchler did not indeed publish a Vivaldi concerto, but composed a concerto of his own in Baroque style, written in the 20th Century: it is thus entirely legitimate to play the concerto with Küchler's own phrasing and articulation, ideally from the piano part.

Beginning of 1st movement with Küchler's articulation, bars 1–8, violin part

The original edition of 1937 contains numerous inconsistencies and errors, some relating to bowing and articulation markings in the violin part, along with numerous discrepancies between the solo part and the violin part printed above the score. For example, in Küchler's score the lyrical middle section of the first movement (bars 33–39) is shown without *portato* markings. In the solo part, however, the *portato* markings in the main theme in the older edition have been added to this lyrical section, too.

Such inconsistencies were one reason for preparing this new edition. A further aim was to pare down the score, presenting notation better suited to the Baroque style and giving teachers and students scope for their own creative interpretation.

Peter Mohrs
Translation Julia Rushworth

Hinweise für den Unterricht

Innerhalb der vier Concertinos von Küchler ragt das Concertino op. 15 „im Stil von Antonio Vivaldi" schon alleine wegen seines Kompositionsstiles heraus. Bedient sich Küchler bei den anderen Schülerkonzerten der klassisch-romantischen Tonsprache, schreibt er hier ein Werk in barockem Stil, das in großen Teilen tatsächlich aus der Feder des Komponisten Vivaldi stammen könnte.

Schon beim Thema des 1. Satzes (*Allegro moderato*) ist die Anlehnung an das berühmte Konzert in a-Moll op. 3/6 des italienischen Komponisten- und Violinlehrerkollegen sofort spürbar: Tonwiederholungen prägen das Thema beider Violinkonzerte. Parallelen gibt es auch hinsichtlich der Form, mit dem für Vivaldi typischen Wechsel eines wiederkehrenden Ritornells mit solistischen Teilen. Auch die vielen spielfreudigen Sechzehntel-Läufe atmen ganz den Geist Vivaldis. In diesen Läufen wird neben der 1. Lage an einigen Stellen auch die 3. Lage verlangt. Auch wenn im Titel der Erstausgabe der Hinweis „1. & 3. Lage" explizit enthalten ist, kann alternativ durchaus auch einmal die 2. Lage sinnvoll sein, so in Takt 29 des 1. Satzes, aber auch an einigen Stellen des langsamen Satzes. Die Beherrschung der ersten drei Griffarten, flinke Finger sowie engagierter Bogenstrich werden vorausgesetzt.

In wunderbarem Kontrast dazu steht der langsame 2. Satz (*Larghetto*) mit dem wiegenden 6/8-Takt eines Sicilianos. Er enthält ebenfalls einige Stellen in der 3. Lage und rückt wegen der vielen ruhigen Bindungen und dem erforderlichen gesanglichen Spiel den Fokus mehr auf den Bogenarm und die tonliche Gestaltung.

Der 3. Satz (*Allegro assai*) ist ein spritziges, spielfreudiges Rondo im 3/8-Takt, bei dem eine deutliche Betonung der ersten Zählzeiten zu beachten ist. Auch hier gibt es mehrere Stellen in der 3. Lage, denen man besondere Aufmerksamkeit schenken sollte. Das Rondo verlangt zudem eine gute Geläufigkeit und ein lockeres rechtes Handgelenk.

Ferdinand Küchler hat die Violinstimme in seinem Concertino „im Stile von Antonio Vivaldi" sehr genau mit Artikulationshinweisen versehen und dabei vor allem Portatostriche und Staccati verwendet. Das war die Sichtweise des ausgehenden 19. und beginnenden 20. Jahrhunderts. Die Frage, wie die Musik der Barockzeit interpretiert und gespielt werden soll, hat im Laufe der Zeit verschiedene Antworten erfahren und unterliegt in gewissem Sinne der Mode und dem interpretatorischen Zeitgeist. Heute, auf der Basis der Erkenntnisse der historischen Aufführungspraxis, wird man manches anders spielen als zur Zeit Küchlers. Daher hat sich die vorliegende Neuausgabe dafür entschieden, die Artikulationen von Küchler nicht abzudrucken und viel-

mehr der sparsameren Notationspraxis der Barockzeit zu folgen, um einen unvoreingenommen Zugang zu dieser Musik zu ermöglichen. Auch wurden einige Bogenstriche und Fingersätze ergänzt.

Natürlich muss man sich aber auch der Tatsache bewusst sein, dass Küchler kein Vivaldi-Konzert herausgegeben hat, sondern im 20. Jahrhundert ein eigenes Konzert im barocken Stil komponierte. Es ist also ebenso legitim, das Konzert mit Küchlers Phrasierung und Artikulation (bevorzugt aus der Klavierstimme) zu spielen.

Anfang des 1. Satzes mit Küchlers Artikulation, T. 1–8, Violinstimme

Die Originalausgabe von 1937 enthält zahlreiche Inkonsequenzen und Fehler, einerseits was die Logik der Striche und Artikulationen in der Violinstimme betrifft, andererseits mit Blick auf die zahlreichen Abweichungen zwischen der Solostimme und der in der Partitur überlegten Violinstimme. Küchler hat z.B. den lyrischen Mittelteil des 1. Satzes (T. 33–39) in der Partitur ohne Portato-Striche notiert. In der Einzelstimme aber wurden die Portato-Striche des Hauptthemas in der alten Ausgabe stereotyp auch auf diesen lyrischen Teil übertragen.

Diese und andere Ungereimtheiten waren ein Grund für die vorliegende Neuausgabe. Ein weiterer Grund war der Wunsch, den Notentext zu entschlacken, mehr an die barocke Stilistik anzupassen sowie Lehrer und Schüler Platz für eigene kreative Ideen zu geben.

Peter Mohrs

Indications pour l'apprentissage

Le concertino op. 15 « dans le style d'Antonio Vivaldi » se démarque d'emblée des trois autres concertinos de Küchler, ne serait-ce que par le style d'écriture employé. En effet, si dans les autres concertinos Küchler utilise le langage classique-romantique, il livre avec celui-ci une œuvre composée dans le style baroque dont Vivaldi pourrait, en grande partie, être l'auteur.

Dès le thème du 1er mouvement (*Allegro moderato*), la référence au célèbre concerto en la mineur op. 3/6 de son collègue compositeur et professeur de violon italien est immédiatement sensible : les thèmes des deux concertos pour violons comprennent tous deux des notes répétées. Des parallèles existent aussi sur le plan formel avec l'alternance d'une ritournelle récurrente et de passages de nature plus solistique caractéristique de Vivaldi. Les nombreux traits de doubles-croches si agréables à jouer respirent aussi totalement l'esprit vivaldien. Outre la première position, il arrive que ces traits fassent également appel à la troisième position. Par ailleurs, même si le titre de la première édition contient expressément la mention « 1re et 3e position », la 2e position peut aussi parfois avoir du sens en guise d'alternative, par exemple mesure 29 du 1er mouvement ou en quelques endroits du mouvement lent. La maîtrise des trois premières positions, l'agilité des doigts ainsi qu'un archet engagé sont des présupposés.

Bercé par la mesure à 6/8 d'une sicilienne, le 2e mouvement (*Larghetto*) constitue un merveilleux contraste par rapport au précédent. Ce mouvement lent contient également des passages en 3e position. Du fait de la sérénité induite par les nombreuses liaisons et de la nécessité d'adopter un jeu chantant, l'attention s'y concentre davantage sur le bras de l'archet et la construction du son.

Le 3e mouvement (*Allegro assai*) est un rondo gai et agréable à jouer en 3/8 pour lequel le premier temps sera nettement accentué. Il comporte aussi plusieurs passages en 3e position auxquels il faudra accorder une attention particulière. Le rondo nécessite également une bonne aisance et un poignet droit bien souple.

Ferdinand Küchler a pourvu la partie de violon solo de son concertino « dans le style d'Antonio Vivaldi » d'indications d'articulation très précises. Il y utilise avant tout des signes de *portato* et de *staccato*. Cela correspond à la façon de voir de la fin du 19e siècle et du début du 20e siècle. Mais la question de savoir comment la musique baroque doit être interprétée et jouée a fait l'objet de réponses différentes au fil du temps, dépendant jusqu'à un certain point de la mode et de la perception des problématiques liées à l'interprétation. Aujourd'hui, sur la base des découvertes relatives aux pratiques historiques,

certaines choses seront jouées différemment qu'elles ne l'étaient à l'époque de Küchler. C'est pourquoi cette nouvelle édition a décidé de ne pas reproduire les indications d'articulation de Küchler, mais au contraire, de se conformer à la sobriété de la notation de l'époque baroque afin de permettre un accès à cette musique libre de toute idée préconçue. Quelques coups d'archet et des doigtés ont également été ajoutés.

Évidemment, il faut bien être conscients du fait que Küchler n'a pas publié un concerto de Vivaldi, mais un concerto dans le style baroque composé par ses soins au 20e siècle. Il est donc aussi parfaitement légitime de jouer ce concerto avec le phrasé et les articulations de Küchler, (idéalement tirés de la partie pour piano).

Début du 1er mouvement avec l'articulation de Küchler, mes. 1 à 8, violon

L'édition originale de 1937 contient de nombreuses erreurs et incohérences relevant d'une part de la logique des coups d'archet et de l'articulation dans la partie de violon, et d'autre part des nombreuses divergences entre la partition séparée de violon solo et la voix de violon solo figurant dans le conducteur. Par exemple, dans ce dernier, Küchler note la partie centrale chantante du 1er mouvement (mes. 33–39) sans signes de *portato*. Cependant, dans la partition séparée du soliste de l'ancienne édition, les signes de *portato* du thème principal ont été ajoutés automatiquement au-dessus de cette partie chantante.

Ces incohérences sont l'une des raisons de la présente nouvelle édition. Une autre raison tient au souhait d'élaguer la partition, de la rapprocher davantage du style baroque et également de ménager de l'espace afin que les professeurs et leurs élèves puisse exprimer leurs propres idées créatives.

Peter Mohrs
Traduction Michaëla Rubi